THE BLACK MAMBA

BY LISA OWINGS

BELLWETHER MEDIA • MINNEAPOLIS, MN

Jump into the cockpit and take flight with Pilot books. Your journey will take you on high-energy adventures as you learn about all that is wild, weird, fascinating, and fun!

This edition first published in 2013 by Bellwether Media, Inc.

No part of this publication may be reproduced in whole or in part without written permission of the publisher. For information regarding permission, write to Bellwether Media, Inc., Attention: Permissions Department, 5357 Penn Avenue South, Minneapolis, MN 55419.

Library of Congress Cataloging-in-Publication Data

Owings, Lisa.
  The black mamba / by Lisa Owings.
    pages cm. – (Pilot. Nature's deadliest)
Audience: 8-12.
Includes bibliographical references and index.
 Summary: "Fascinating images accompany information about the black mamba. The combination of high-interest subject matter and narrative text is intended for students in grades 3 through 7" –Provided by publisher.
  ISBN 978-1-60014-877-4 (hardcover : alk. paper)
 1. Black mamba–Juvenile literature. I. Title.
 QL666.O64O93 2013
 597.96/4–dc23
                                    2012035841

Printed in the United States of America, North Mankato, MN.

CONTENTS

Brush with a Black Mamba

It was a day like any other in the East African country of Tanzania. Ernest, a young Maasai warrior, was working with friends to herd the tribe's cattle. He took this task seriously. He knew the Maasai people could not survive without their cattle. As Ernest walked next to the herd, he saw one of the cows break away and run off. He began to chase after it.

Suddenly, a flash of dark scales stopped Ernest in his tracks. He had stepped dangerously close to a black mamba. His first instinct was to run, but it was too late for that. The furious mamba struck before Ernest could move a muscle.

Danger in Africa

About 20,000 Africans die from snake bites each year. Black mambas are responsible for many of these deaths.

Ernest felt the snake's fangs sink into his leg. Then the mamba slithered down a hole and out of sight. Ernest knew most black mamba bites resulted in death. He had to act quickly if he was going to survive. Luckily, he knew exactly what to do.

Ernest sat down under a nearby tree. He tied a rope tightly above the bite wound. This was a risky move. The rope could cut off his blood supply and cause him to lose his leg. But it would also help keep the venom from spreading. Ernest was prepared to sacrifice his leg to stay alive.

Ernest rested beneath the tree while his friend ran to get a motorbike. The bike was their only way to get help in time. Ernest's friend soon returned and they rode to the clinic at Meserani Snake Park. On the way, Ernest lost feeling in his leg. His bare foot slipped off the footrest and dragged along the ground. Then everything went dark.

Ernest woke up two days later. His vision was blurry and his foot was torn up. But he was alive against all odds. His doctors had to give him nine doses of antivenom to save his life. And he hadn't lost his leg after all. Ernest gradually recovered under his doctors' care. He was ready to go home just two weeks after his brush with a black mamba.

Milking the Mamba

Black mamba venom is needed to make life-saving antivenom. Trained experts risk their lives to "milk" these fearsome snakes. They grab the snake just behind its head. Then they press its fangs over a container to collect the venom.

Shadow of Death

Many people believe the black mamba is the deadliest snake in the world. Some call it the Shadow of Death. It is found only in Africa, where people live in fear of its **fatal** bite. This nightmarish snake is thin but strong. It can grow more than 10 feet (3 meters) in length. When it is ready to strike, it raises the front part of its body off the ground. The longest black mambas can look a human in the eye before attacking.

Africa

human

black mamba

black mamba territory = ▢

N
W E
S

Ernest and Nurse Rarin at Meserani Snake Park

After the Attack

Ernest is herding cattle again. He is now married and ha̶s̶ soon.

Open Wide

The black mamba is not actually black. Its scales are usually gray or brown. The snake is named for the inky black color of its mouth.

The black mamba is faster than any other snake on Earth. It glides over the ground at up to 12.5 miles (20 kilometers) per hour. Its strike is also lightning-quick. It hits its target with deadly **accuracy**. The black mamba's fangs are positioned to pierce its victims at the slightest touch.

Be Afraid

A single black mamba can move a whole herd of large animals. All it has to do is raise its head above the grass and open its mouth. The herd scatters in terror.

The black mamba hunts during the day. Its body forms a series of S-shaped curves as it pushes itself along the ground. It flicks its tongue in and out to sniff the air for signs of prey. Trees and bodies of water won't come between the black mamba and a tasty meal. This snake swims well and climbs easily.

The black mamba often slithers into the burrow or nest of a small animal. It sneaks up on its prey. Then it strikes in a flash. As its fangs pierce the victim's skin, the black mamba **injects** its **potent** venom. The poison kills within minutes. Then the black mamba stretches its jaws around the body. Soon it has swallowed its meal whole.

If a black mamba feels threatened, it usually tries to escape. The snake becomes **aggressive** if it can't get away. It raises its head and flattens out the skin on its neck. This makes the black mamba appear larger. Then it opens its dark mouth and hisses a warning. If the threat doesn't back off, the snake attacks. The black mamba will bite several times to defend itself.

Black mamba venom **paralyzes** muscles. Within minutes, victims feel dizzy and sleepy. They begin to lose control of their bodies. Soon the venom attacks the heart and the muscles used for breathing. Without antivenom, victims cannot survive.

Black Mamba Attacks

Black mambas attack people only in self-defense. They would rather flee than face a human. However, they are fierce fighters when surprised or cornered. It is important to be extremely careful when in black mamba territory.

Wear boots and long pants if you must enter black mamba habitats. Move slowly and watch carefully for movement on the ground. It is best to travel in a group. This way you can look out for one another and get help if needed.

Home Sweet Home

Black mambas live on grassy plains and rocky hills. They often make homes in termite mounds or hollow trees. Sometimes they find their way into people's houses when hunting rats or mice.

If you see a black mamba, back away slowly. Sudden movements can startle it into attacking. If the snake feels threatened, it will rear up and hiss. Calmly and quickly back away if this happens. Make sure the snake has a way to escape. Warn others in the area of the snake's presence.

A black mamba's strike can be too quick to see. Its bite can be almost painless. It is important to stay alert in black mamba territory. If you think you have been bitten, every minute counts. Your life depends on getting to a hospital quickly. Call ahead to let the staff know you will need black mamba antivenom.

On the Way

Take steps to slow the spread of black mamba venom while on the way to the hospital.

- Do your best to stay calm and still.

- Wrap a bandage tightly around the bitten limb.

- Keep the limb below your heart if possible.

Attack Facts

- Without treatment, black mamba bites are 100 percent fatal.

- The black mamba's fast-acting venom can kill a human within 20 minutes.

- Each black mamba bite injects enough venom to kill more than ten people.

Victims of black mamba attacks have a good chance of surviving if they receive antivenom quickly. However, there are many places in Africa where antivenom is not available. Additionally, many snakebite victims have no way to get to a hospital soon enough. People in Africa are so afraid of black mambas that they often kill these powerful snakes. Experts know black mambas bite only when threatened. They want to help people understand these skilled predators to save the lives of both. It is natural to fear the Shadow of Death, but the black mamba also deserves our respect.

Swaziland Saint

Thea Litschka-Koen teaches people in Swaziland about black mambas and other deadly snakes. She also rescues hundreds of snakes each year and relocates them to safer places.

aggressive—violent or threatening

antivenom—a substance that acts against venom and treats the effects of a venomous bite

fangs—the pointed teeth of venomous snakes; fangs are hollow or grooved to guide venom into prey.

fatal—resulting in death

injects—inserts fluid into the body through a sharp point; a black mamba injects venom through its fangs.

paralyzes—causes the loss of movement or feeling

potent—very powerful or strong

sacrifice—to give up or do without

venom—poison produced by some animals to kill or paralyze prey

To Learn More

At the Library

Blobaum, Cindy. *Awesome Snake Science: 40 Activities For Learning About Snakes*. Chicago, Ill.: Chicago Review Press, 2012.

Howard, Melanie A. *Black Mambas*. Mankato, Minn.: Capstone Press, 2012.

Laita, Mark. *Serpentine*. New York, N.Y.: Abrams, 2013.

On the Web

Learning more about black mambas is as easy as 1, 2, 3.

1. Go to www.factsurfer.com.

2. Enter "black mambas" into the search box.

3. Click the "Surf" button and you will see a list of related Web sites.

With factsurfer.com, finding more information is just a click away.

Index